HA HA HA

HA HA HA

HA HA

HA HA HA

HA

Arkham Asylum

MADNESS

Written and
drawn by
Sam Kieth

Colors by **Michelle Madsen**
and **Dave Stewart**

Painted pages by **Sam Kieth**

Letters by **Steve Wands**

Batman created by **Bob Kane**

Michael Siglain Editor
Harvey Richards Assistant Editor
Robbin Brosterman Design Director-Books
Louis Prandi Art Director

DC COMICS
Diane Nelson President
Dan DiDio and Jim Lee Co-Publishers
Geoff Johns Chief Creative Officer
Patrick Caldon EVP-Finance and Administration
John Rood EVP-Sales, Marketing and Business Development
Amy Genkins SVP-Business and Legal Affairs
Steve Rotterdam SVP-Sales and Marketing
John Cunningham VP-Marketing
Terri Cunningham VP-Managing Editor
Alison Gill VP-Manufacturing
David Hyde VP-Publicity
Sue Pohja VP-Book Trade Sales
Alysse Soll VP-Advertising and Custom Publishing
Bob Wayne VP-Sales
Mark Chiarello Art Director

ARKHAM ASYLUM: MADNESS
Published by DC Comics, 1700 Broadway, New York, NY 10019.
Copyright © 2010 by DC Comics. All rights reserved. All characters,
the distinctive likenesses thereof and all related elements, are trademarks
of DC Comics. The stories, characters and incidents mentioned in this
book are entirely fictional. DC Comics does not read or accept unsolicited
submissions of ideas, stories or artwork. Printed by RR Donnelley,
Salem, VA, USA. 5/13/11 . First Printing. DC Comics, a Warner Bros.
Entertainment Company.
ISBN: 978-1-4012-2338-0

--MOMMY WORKS IN A NICE PLACE. SHE HELPS PEOPLE GET BETTER. WE NEED TO LEARN COMPASSION FOR THE PEOPLE MOMMY HELPS.

'KAY, MOM. 'BYE.

HEY, IS THAT THE PRETTIEST NURSE AT ARKHAM?

SIGH

CLAK CLAK CLAK CLAK CLAK CLAK CLAK CLAK

Arkham Sign-I	Time In
Sunday	
Monday	
Tuesday	X
Wednesday	
Thursday	
Friday	
Saturday	

Nice, hypocrite. But what can I say?

He's a child.

And with one stroke of lead...

Dayshift's head doctor, Dr. Hurd.

Real hard-ass. Anal. Petty.

Dr. Reed's not as bad. She's mostly dayshift, sometimes works nights for overtime.

Workaholic. Secretive. Defensive—but who in here isn't?

Then the guards: Randy says they take the worst of it, burn out fastest. The faces always change.

The chubby one's the new guy; Randy gives him a week.

Eddy, in the basement, reminds me of my grandfather.

My *other* brick.

Always forget the cleaning woman's name. She brings up the rear, mops up what nobody else will.

And Randy? She tells it like it is. And the best jokes!

Especially the dirty ones.

It's moist up here. Sticky. Humid. Stifling.

SEE, ROY? I WAS TELLIN' YA-- THE *KILLER* HIMSELF. ALMOST NOBODY'S ALLOWED UP HERE.

MAN! FREAKY! SO HOW BIG IS THIS TANK?

5,000 GALLONS. HUGE STRAIN ON THE CONCRETE, BEING TOP FLOOR 'N ALL.

THEY SHOULD'A PUT IT ON THE GROUND FLOOR.

TYPICAL ARKHAM. WACKO DESIGN. WHOLE BUILDING'S A HOUSE OF CARDS; WONDER IT STAYS UP.

WHAT'S THAT ON HIS MOUTH?

YOU'LL BE THANKFUL FOR THAT THING WHEN IT COMES TIME TO FEED 'IM.

CREEPY. HE ALWAYS STAYS UNDERWATER?

YEP.

SO WHO FEEDS HIM?

WE DRAW STRAWS.

OKAY, HONEY. MOMMY WILL SEE YOU AT LUNCH. DON'T FORGET THE BYE-BYE.

ROBBINS, WE NEED TO TALK.

MOMMA'S GOTTA GO. BYE-BYE, HONEY.

DID YOU ASK DR. HURD ABOUT...

NO DICE. WE'RE SHORT-STAFFED AS IT IS. YOU GET OFF AT SEVEN LIKE EVERYONE ELSE.

PLEEEZZ, DR. REED?

WHOA! WHAT'S THAT *BANGING*?

THERE ARE *THREE ROOMS* NURSES SHOULD STAY AWAY FROM: ONE IS THE "AQUARIUM"; SECOND IS THE JOKER'S ROOM; AND THIRD IS *THAT* ROOM. NOW BACK TO WORK.

SIGH... YES, DR. REED.

Ten? Ten-thirty? The light says so.

The doctors encourage hobbies for the inmates.

Hurd encourages it. He's new, so he finds it quaint. Harmless.

THERE'S A LINEAGE TO THESE THINGS, YOU KNOW. JOKES. NOVELTIES. PARLOR GAMES. THE IDIOTS DOWNSTAIRS CALL THEM "ANTIQUES." *HEH.*

Collectibles can teach you a lot about yourself.

Dr. Hurd says I'm becoming a better person because of them.

ere's
ething
side.

They can
feel it.
Everyone
can.

An
obstruction
slowing the
gears.

EDDY, YOU
KNOW WHAT
YOU'VE GOT
TO DO.

By noon, there's a
little spot on the
floor. That's
where I lay them
out, admire them.

Some go
back to
the '20s
and '30s.

Exploding cigars,
eyes that fall out
of glassses... But
my favorite is
"blood soap"--
quite hysterical.

An
ordinary
bar of
soap...

...that turns
red when it
gets wet.

'Course,
you'd
have to
be there.

SHE AIN'T SO BAD. SHE'S WORKIN' THE CRAP JOB OF TRYING TO KEEP THE RATS FROM SWIMMIN' OFF THE ONE PIECE OF DRIFTWOOD THAT'S STILL AFLOAT.

CLOSE YOUR EYES. FEEL THAT BREEZE? THINK OF YOUR LITTLE GUY-- CAN YOU FEEL HIM?

WHAT'S THAT IN THE BOTTOM? SOME SORT OF...

PLAQUE. DON'T KNOW THE FULL STORY. THIS TUB USED TO BE IN THE INMATES' REC YARD.

MILTON NAPIER

SOME "INCIDENT" BETWEEN AN INMATE AND A GUARD GOT UGLY.

OVER A STUPID PLAQUE?

WHICH INMATE?

GET HIM INTO THE INFIRMARY, STAT!

IT'S HIM!-- THE ONE YOU WERE TELLING ME ABOUT. WHAT HAPPENED?

DAMN FOOL KEEPS BUSTING HIS OWN LIGHTBULBS.

OH, RANDY--WHAT'S THAT IN HIS TEETH?

GUESS.

Infirmary, 4:30 pm

MINOR LACERATIONS TO THE INNER CHEEK. HE CHEWED IT. SMART ENOUGH NOT TO SWALLOW.

The things one has to do for a little fresh air.

DISTURBING. A CRY FOR HELP?

WHO KNOWS WITH THIS GUY. IF I HAD A DIME FOR EVERY GUARD THIS MANIAC'S MESSED UP...

STAFF LUNCH

HMM. WELL, *THAT'S* INTERESTING...

THUMP

TIC

THUMP

TIC

THUMP

THUMP

TIC

TIC

THUMP

TIC

THUMP

THUMP

HOME AGAIN, HOME AGAIN, HA-HA-*HA*.

WHOSE CELL IS BEHIND THAT WALL? MAYBE ONE OF THE INMATES IS SCREWIN' WITH US.

THERE'S NO CELL OUTSIDE THIS WALL. I SAY IT'S A CRITTER.

MAYBE THE JOKER STUCK SOMETHIN' IN THERE. A FINGER? TOE?

I'm guessing it's just after 5:00, the way the light's disappearing from above.

Just enough time to admire my collectibles once more before the sun slips away...

...for good.

WHAT'S IN HERE??

USE YOUR HEAD. HOW WOULD THE JOKER--OR ANYONE--GET UP THERE?

ENOUGH ABOUT THE CLOCK. THERE'S ENOUGH TO DO BEFORE THE NIGHT CREW COMES ON. LET'S JUST STICK A FORK IN THIS DAY.

WHAT'S THE MATTER WITH ROY?

GOT DUMPED.

TIC

THUMP

THUMP

THUMP

TIC

TIC

TIC

THUMP

THUMP THUMP

TIC

TIC

THUMP

THUMP THUMP

TIC

SNIFF

PEGGY, OH PEGGY...

TIC

TIC

TIC

TIC

HEY, RANDY, IT'S ALMOST SEVEN, AND THEN WE'RE OFF--THANK GOSH! NEVER THOUGHT THIS DAY WOULD END.

HEY-- WHAT'S WITH THE BOX?

LISTEN, SABINE--SNIFF-- YOU MAY AS WELL KNOW, I JUST FOUND OUT...THIS IS MY LAST DAY.

YOU QUITTING???

FIRED.

OH, RANDY-- YOU CAN'T LEAVE ME! YOU'RE THE ONLY ONE AROUND HERE WHO KEEPS ME COMING BACK. I'LL TALK TO THE DOCTORS; THEY'VE GOTTA KEEP YOU ON!

TOO LATE, KIDDO. STUPID CLICHE: DOCTOR PLAYS HANKY-PANKY WITH THE NURSE, THEN DROPS HER WHEN THINGS GET "COMPLICATED."

NO--I WON'T LET THEM! YOU'RE COMING IN TOMORROW.

NO, I'M NOT. MAYBE IT'S FOR THE BEST. ANY PLACE IS BETTER THAN THIS HELLHOLE.

AWWW--DON'T START--YOU'RE ALMOST OFF-SHIFT, REMEMBER?

BUT TOMORROW...

TOMORROW YOU'LL COME IN, JUST LIKE EVERY MORNING, AND ONE DAY YOU'LL BE A "RANDY" TO SOME NEWBIE NURSE, AND YOU'LL BE THE ONE CRACKING JOKES AND TOUGHENING HER UP.

SMOOCH

THE DOCTOR WHO DID IT ASSURED ME IT'S...NOTHING PERSONAL.

SAME DOCTOR WHO CALLED ME SNUGGLEBUNCH IN THE SUPPLY CLOSET.

SNUGGLEBUNCH?? HURD IS SUCH A JERK!

IT'S NOT HURD, SWEETIE. IT'S REED...

REED?

WELL! I'M GONNA MARCH OVER THERE AND FIX THIS RIGHT NOW!

SABINE, WAIT--

YOU'D DO IT IF IT WERE ME. NOW HUSH.

CLIC CLIC CLICCLI

YOO HOO--DR. REED!

CLIC CLIC CLIC CLI

SLAM

SABINE, I'M IN THE MIDDLE--

THIS STINKS!

WHAT?

DEFLOWERING YOUR NURSES... AND THEN *FIRING* THEM WHEN YOU'VE DECIDED TO MOVE ON. RANDY HAS A LIFE, BILLS, RENT. I'D'VE EXPECTED THIS FROM A *MALE*, LIKE DR. HURD--

RANDY WASN'T FIRED FOR... PERSONAL REASONS.

YOU EXPECT ME TO BELIEVE THAT?

I DON'T CARE; IT'S NONE OF YOUR BUSINESS. NOW GO BACK TO WORK.

WHAT IF I TELL?

IT'LL FALL ON DEAF EARS.

Nobody cares. Everybody sleeps with everybody around here. Any excuse to... escape.

SABINE, YOU CAN PAINT ME AS COLD-HEARTED AS YOU WANT, BUT RANDY'S A BIG GIRL. SHE DIDN'T WANT TO FACE THE FACT THAT SHE WASN'T CUTTING IT. SHE TRIED TO USE "US" TO HOLD ONTO A JOB SHE SHOULD'VE BEEN FIRED FROM YEARS AGO. HAS IT OCCURRED TO YOU THAT SHE USED ME?

UHH... RANDY WOULD NEVER...

BY THE WAY, NOW THAT SHE'S GON[E] YOU HAVE TO WORK T[HE] NIGHT SHIFT, TOO.

WHAT??? NO WAY!!

NO CHOICE. ONLY TWO NURSES COVERING FOUR POSTS TONIGHT. I'LL PAY YOU OVERTIME. IF YOU SAY NO, YOU'RE FIRED, TOO. AGREED?

YOU *KNOW* I HAVE NO CHOICE. I CAN'T MAKE IT WITHOUT THIS JOB.

I WON'T FORGET IT. SABINE--BELIEVE IT OR NOT, ASKING YOU TO DO THIS... WASN'T PERSONAL, EITHER.

Night staff,
7:30 pm

And so it begins again. Dr. Gallagher is harmless...just a funny little man with big glasses.

The night staff didn't know about the clock. Now, instead of little drops of blood...

...it's really starting to smell putrid.

Nobody talks about it. The evening crew is much less chatty...and more on edge.

Dr. Williams seems *okay.*

Anyone's better than Reed.

I think these are different guards, but I can't focus anymore. Faces blur. The other two nurses are just two more miserable women trying to survive 'til daylight.

No night cleaning woman...

...no orderlies tonight...

...leaving just the nurses to mop up blood and urine.

ONLY ONE THING'S GONNA GET ME THROUGH THIS--GONNA PULL ME THROUGH THIS *MADNESS...*

...MY OZZIE.

THIS...*SHOE*... HAS COME TO MY ATTENTION. I WAS TOLD THE DAY STAFF WAS USING IT FOR PRACTICAL JOKES.

-:SIGH:- DOES ANYBODY KNOW WHERE IT CAME FROM?

SOMEBODY FOUND IT IN THE REC ROOM, SIR. IT'S JUST A JOKE, THOUGH.

IT IS NOT A JOKE. DR. REED BECAME SUSPICIOUS AND SENT SAMPLES TO A LAB. THIS IS AN *ACTUAL HUMAN FOOT* SOAKED IN FORMALDEHYDE AND LACQUERED TO LOOK LIKE A PROP. THIS FOOT BELONGED TO BEN POLITO.

YEAH--I REMEMBER THAT GUY!

RIGHT-- HE *DID* LOSE HIS LEG! BUT WHY WOULD HE DO THIS TO IT?

An open cell door. That's not good...

THIS LOOKS LIKE THE JOKER'S CELL. BUT... WHY IS IT DARK?

WHAT'S THAT ON THE FLOOR?

WHY... *CREAM,* MY DEAR.

"SHAVING," TO BE EXACT.

AS TO WHY IT'S DARK, I THINK YOU'D BETTER ASK DR. HURD.

OH, GOD!

IS THAT *SHOCKED EXPRESSION* YOUR RESPONSE TO BEING ALONE WITH *THE CLOWN PRINCE OF CRIME?* OR...

PLOP

In the basement, the pipes creak...

...and swell.

No one's listening.

Everyone's braced.

The people,

the bricks,

the mortar--

It's like it's all going to implode.

HAS to.

BEEN WORKING HERE 20 YEARS--PLACE AIN'T *HAUNTED.* AND THE FRIGGIN' WALLS AIN'T *"BLEEDING."*

I'M GONNA GET UP THERE MYSELF AND HAND-SCRUB THAT BLASTED WALL *CLEAN.* BUT FIRST...I GOTTA GET *UP* THERE.

HEY, EDDY--THAT'S ONE HONKIN' LADDER!

JUST BOUGHT IT, DOC. EXTRA LONG.

YAY! EDDY'S GONNA BREAK *THE CURSE OF THE BLEEDING CLOCK.* IS IT EVEN WORKING, STILL?

BARELY. ALL THE LADDERS AROUND HERE ARE TOO DAMN SHORT. DON'T KNOW HOW THEY GOT UP THERE IN THE FIRST PLACE. 'COURSE, A LOT OF THINGS AROUND HERE...

YOU ALL FORGET I WORK IN THE BASEMENT. EVERY INCH OF THAT RUSTY, CORRODED OLD DUNGEON IS THE *BOWELS* OF THIS PLACE.

INMATES USED TO BREAK OUT THROUGH THE VENTS, SO WE PUT IN NEW ONES, SMALLER ONES.

THEY USED TO TRY TO SNEAK OUT BETWEEN THE WALLS, OR THROUGH THE SEWAGE. WE BARRED THOSE UP, TOO.

DRIP

DRIP CREEK

DRIP

DRIP

CREEK DRIP

YEAH, IT'S OLD. OVERLOADED. RUN-DOWN, SOMETIMES HANGING BY A THREAD.

So am I. Maybe everyone who works here is--especially at night.

YOU GUYS MARK MY WORDS-- WE'RE OVER THE HUMP WITH THIS MOUSE THING. ONLY A FEW HOURS LEFT 'TIL THE DAY CREW TAKES OVER AND WE'RE...

uess."

HOLY CRAP!! WHERE'S ALL THIS COMING FROM???

WOOSSHH

CRACK CRACK CRM

OH, GREAT-- CROC'S TANK MUST'VE BLOWN. IT'S GONNA FLOOD DOWN EACH OF THE FLOORS. WE GOTTA GET EVERYONE OFF THE FIFTH FLOOR NOW!

CCREEEKK CCREEK REEK

CRASH

Listen to the walls! This whole place may collapse.

NOW WHAT? IS THAT... WATER?

IT'S THE TANK! EVERYONE ON THE FIRST FLOOR--OUT OF THE BUILDING! NOW!

EDDY, TAKE THE ORDERLIES, AND ROUND UP THE INMATES! EDDY? WHERE'S EDDY?? OH, MAN--EVERY- THING'S GOING TO...

HEY, SABINE. DIDN'T THINK I'D SEE *YOU* BACK HERE.

YOU EITHER. YOU DIDN'T QUIT?

CARRIED MY RESIGNATION LETTER AROUND FOR AN HOUR BEFORE TURNING IT IN. JUST SAYING GOODBYE NOW.

YOU?

I TYPED ONE UP, TOO. I WISH... ROY, I'VE GOT A KID. A HUSBAND...

IT'S SO WEIRD... TO LOOK AT THIS TUB, KNOWING WHAT JOKER DID TO THAT GUY IN IT.

REMEMBER WHEN JOKER SAID I MUST BE A MASOCHIST FOR STAYING HERE?

IS THAT IT? YOUR LETTER?

YEP. TO TURN IT IN.. OR...

YEAH-- *THAT'S* THE QUESTION. MAYBE I'M A COWARD; I TURNED MINE IN *BEFORE* I HAD A CHANCE TO THINK ABOUT IT.

MAYBE YOU'RE BRAVE-- OR JUST *REALISTIC.*

WHEN I CAME HERE, I SWORE I WOULDN'T WIND UP LIKE EVERYONE ELSE. IT'S LIKE THIS PLACE IS *ALIVE,* ROY ARKHAM; THE BUILDING-- *EVERYTHING.* WE DON'T EVEN THINK FOR OURSELVES; WE JUST EXPRESS ALL THIS...

MADNESS?

LISTEN, SABINE--I'VE GOT TO GO. YOU SHOULDN'T TAKE YOUR BREAKS HERE, BY "OLD RED."

THAT WATER'S SO DIRTY, YOU CAN'T SEE...KNOWING WHAT HAPPENED, IT'S *BAD LUCK* TO STARE INTO THAT TUB.

GOODBYE, SABINE.

As she drives away, I can feel that she is taking part of me with her. They all do.

When things go awry, you can scrub the walls, haul the bloody tub to the field, mop up, clean and power-wash, rebuild, sanitize feverishly... You can get all the nastiness out. Or try. They **always** try.

But I'm still there, **inside them.** Diluting their dreams, nightmares, and hopes, every minute of the day. Not just the Asylum's horror...

...a very personal, **ordinary bloodshed.** What they **settle** for. What they **abandon** themselves to.

And for **whom.**

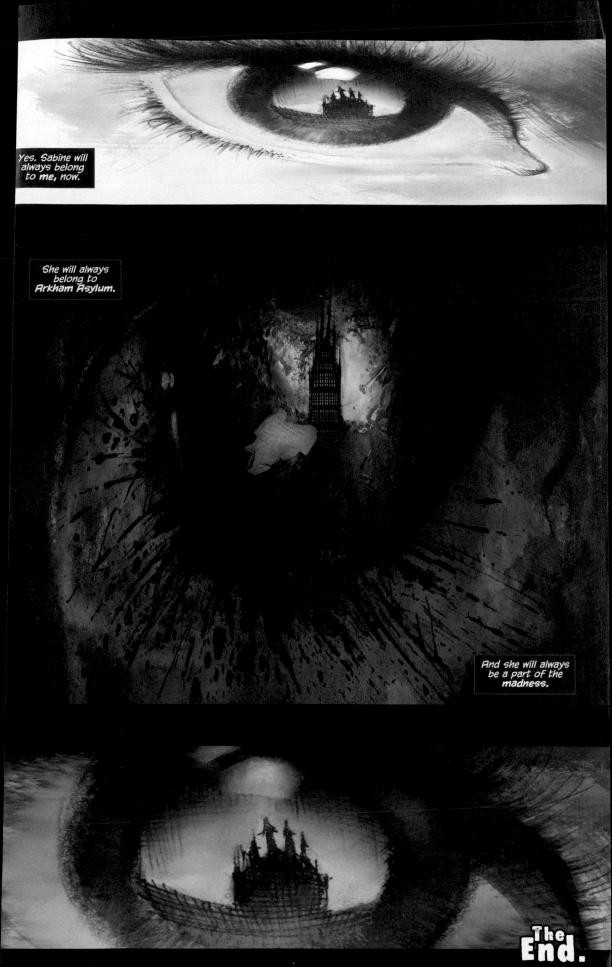

Yes. Sabine will always belong to me, now.

She will always belong to *Arkham Asylum.*

And she will always be a part of the madness.

The End.

Arkham Afterwards

Arkham was the last of four projects I finished for DC, including the Batman Confidential run, the Scott Ian Lobo books, and a Batman Mad Hatter Hardcover project Bruce Jones wrote which I started first, but will probably be released last. Arkham was the last project I drew and it turned out more ambitious, both in painter material, being long form, 97 pages, and in what became an elaborate and detailed collaboration with editor Mike Siglain. I often joked that Mike should be given co-plotter credit, as he had as strong a vision of this Haunted House book as I did. He provided probably more freedom than anyone I've worked with, yet kept pushing me to push myself to "go farther," artistically and creatively.

The phenomenal contributions of colorists Dave Stewart and Michelle Madsen cannot be overstated. However, as for myself, while I'm overall... satisfied with MOST of what I've written and drawn, the techniques I used, much more collage, computer and photo manipulation colliding with hand-painted art, are mixed at best. The problem with digital art seems to be when it draws attention to itself. I decided early on I'd not try to hide my cartoonish hand-drawn style, watercolor or hand-painted art with digital tricks and manipulated photos which are far more realistic than I have the skill to pull off. So, for me the book was an experiment IF these two styles can be merged, without having to fight, distract or apologize for the other. On this level I think it shows the limits of "digital distraction," as in being drawn OUT of a story by the technique, but the same could be true of detailed art. I consider it a brave failure, an ambitious one, but ultimately a good argument why everything I draw after this will probably try to show more organic hand-drawn watercolor in the minimal Chinese brush-painting style or more abstract work, which is the only unexplored place left TO go after all this anal-detail-for-its-own-sake style I milked to death in this book.

Thus, Arkham is a necessary and not altogether unpleasant little dead end. Not only in plot, the dark story ends with the characters not only trapped, staff and inmates, but also, particularly Sabine, the nurse, giving up on herself. It is a choice, a failing we're all vulnerable to. To me that's scarier than any amount of blood, violence or physical carnage. I also was unable to hide my sense of humor, and Mike also encouraged this, God help him.

My two favorite lines in the book — well, my wife, who types it for me, her favorite line was the Joker being dragged away and complaining of missing Antiques Roadshow, whereas my favorite moment was the Joker's narration as he peacefully, almost cheerfully paints the severed foot in craft class.

Like the Joker, I got too carried away on this book, hand-making my own antiques jokes, aging them by computer, printing them out by hand, then spilling red paint "blood" on the box I'd hand-crumpled, all for something that would only appear in a few panels. And that's only one example.

I'd often paint as many as 6 to 15 different versions of a page, a colossal waste of time, energy and sanity, and also proving multiple pages don't always result in a BETTER page, just different. When I painted the Killer Croc page at the beginning of the book on page 9, I said to Siglain, "I'm not sure I can do a technically better splash of Croc than this" and Mike said, "Why not use it as a splash in the back of the book, then work your way up to it with hints at Croc, maybe with small inset panels." I liked this since it HID the fact that I probably could not paint such a successful Croc page, possibly ever again. But, as with the antiques jokes, and dead guards, and ticking clock, I became obsessed, overworking and reworking, and became a WORSE artist, and person, in the process. I, at last, and with Mike's help, had to step back and laugh and have compassion for myself, much as I did with the Joker. Older. Slower. Hopefully wiser.

As I watch myself age DOING this book, and have to laugh at myself, my own folly, I also TRIED to inject some humanity into these carefully guarded franchises we write and draw. I wanted to care about Sabine using her son to get through the day, to care about something in the middle of this hellish mess. Some light in the middle of the madness. To me, in a way it's either a horror story that she crumples her resignation letter, or a testament to her sacrifice for her son that she stays. To me the most chilling line in the book is when the Joker asks why she doesn't quit.

Visually, I'm all over the board and know my distorted and "wonky" view of Batman and the Joker is not for everyone. But thankfully editors like Siglain, Marts, Sattler and Dan DiDio seem to get a twisted thrill out of letting me run bad with their characters every once in a while. Then, like the Joker, I'm shoved back into my little cell and the characters are allowed to look normal again through other artists' safer, saner hands, much to the relief of the majority of fan boys, I am sure. Another dead end.

But reaching a dead end also means an opportunity for something new. Or a chance at it. I am saying goodbye in a way to the last two years at DC, but remember, I told Siglain I'd only take the Arkham job if I could not only top the Joker I drew in Batman: Secrets, but at least do a different take on him, breathe some new life into him…or die trying. So, I tried. I may have missed the mark, but I had fun trying, obsessing, and finally… moving on.

What art you'll see in the back is various raw, unfiltered versions of things, odds and ends, but most of the good stuff is buried between the covers.

sam kieth

Sam Kieth is the umpty-ninth comic artist who's done work for Marvel, DC, Image, and a long list of indie comics publishers. He drew the first five SANDMANs, and created The Maxx in '93, which became an animated series on MTV.

Despite writing bios of himself in the third person, he quietly lives with his wife somewhere in the mountains, writes a series of "trout books" for Oni Press, and wastes too much time making childish things out of duct tape.

This book is dedicated to everyone who hates their job.